THE

SECRET'S

INSIDE

Published by S.O.L. Productions Ltd.
Quarantine Hill, Wicklow, Ireland
email: gabriellekirby@gmail.com

ISBN : 1 90171209 5

Cover Design: Joshua Kelly

THE

SECRET'S

INSIDE

by

Gabrielle Kirby

Published by S.O.L. Productions Ltd.

This book is dedicated to
Monica and Michael Kirby,
my parents.

Foreword

I find it very encouraging to just open a
book, read a little and find myself inspired.
It doesn't always happen, but when it does it
spurs me on to do things I've always wanted
to do, things that were lying dormant in the
recesses of my mind.
Encouragement can come in many ways:
a word, a look, a touch. And we all have
many different needs.
I hope there is something in here for you,
perhaps that encouraging word you were
waiting for, a helping hand to give you a lift
or just a whisper of hope to have another go,
resurrect a dream, plan that trip.

See if any of the reflections touch what is
deepest inside you, unearthing hopes that
were, perhaps, hidden long ago.
You may get the encouragement you need to
go for gold, patch up a relationship, or just
say 'no' without hurting someone.

Enjoy the journey!

Gabrielle Kirby

Amazing

It's amazing what can be achieved
when someone believes in you.
It's even more amazing
what can be achieved
if you just
believe
in
yourself.

Relaxation

Relaxation is a time
for your spirit to roam freely
wherever it wills.
It is a time
for winding down,
eliminating stress
and building your inner life.
You may just feel terrific
after you have relaxed
and that is what matters,
because how you feel
has a big effect on how you operate.

It is very important
to try and have a quiet time
to yourself every day
where there are no disturbances,
no phones
or questions to answer.
Just you on your own
in your own
quiet space.

Heroes

The only difference
between
the hero and the coward
is that the coward gives into fear
whereas the hero overcomes it.
Sometimes we're a coward,
sometimes we're a hero.
We must neither
be depressed by the former
nor elated by the latter.
Let's, however, try
to love what we are
at any
given moment.

Adventure

The road of the positive,
taking a positive attitude to
everything that happens in life,
is one of the most
exciting and adventure-filled
roads one can travel.
You will constantly be challenged
and put to the test,
but if you remain faithful
to only seeing the good side of
every single thing that happens,
both in your world
and in the world of others,
your constant reward will be
happiness
and
peace of mind.

A Secret

One woman's secret
to a happy marriage:
'Laugh a lot
and
never let
the sun go down
on your anger'.

Youth

Sometimes we look at young people
and marvel at their beauty,
energy and vitality.
We attribute these qualities to their youth.
It might be more true to say that the
young are vulnerable
and don't really seem to know it all,
and that's what gives them
their attractiveness.
Add innocence to vulnerability
and the picture is complete.
But are these qualities the prerogative
of the young? I think not.
If we who are 'older' want to get back
our youth and vitality,
we might search for where
we can be more vulnerable,
and there, perhaps, find the life and
energy we're looking for.
This chosen vulnerability may very well
be the essential ingredient in becoming
like a child again,
that special requirement for entering the
state of heaven.

Help

The way things are today,
we have to try to be all things
to all women or men,
as the case may be.
We have to be a father,
a mother,
a psychiatrist, a confessor,
with an endless amount of
compassion and understanding
for everyone
who needs help.
But it's worth it all to be able
to help somebody along the road.
After all, we're all going
in the same direction
and it sure is nice
to give, or get, a helping hand
up the hill of life.

Sorry

When you argue with the one you
love,
it takes time
to muster up the courage
to say sorry.
What does it matter
who's 'right'?
The truth is,
love has stopped
and only resumes
as soon as
one person
makes
the friendly approach.

Perfection

Nobody's perfect,
and although
perfection is not
a bad thing to aim for,
on the way
we are bound to make
mistakes,
blurt out the wrong thing
at the wrong time,
in the wrong place.
As the song says:
'We always hurt the
one we love'.
The only way to cut a diamond is
with another diamond.
With this friction
each is brought
to perfection.

Compassion

A little girl came home
from visiting the house where her
best friend had died.
"Why did you go?"
questioned her father.
"To comfort her mother,"
replied the child.
"And what did you do
to comfort her?"
the father continued.
"I climbed onto her lap
and I cried."

Progress

We can and will make progress
in love and life experience
when we are hurt by the one we love
and try to turn it into profit.
Instead of, perhaps, always wanting
to retaliate or indulge in self-pity.
Take the pain
as a labour of love.
After all, love isn't easy,
we have to work at it and sometimes
take the bad with the good.
Even the bad times can be good
because we get a chance to reflect,
make
positive adjustments
and resolutions for the future,
thereby avoiding the same
unpleasant situation
cropping up
again and again.

Listen

Listening to your inner voice
is
listening to your own
sense of
inner truth.
Your inner voice is all the time
trying to guide you to make
right choices.
Try to tune into your inner
voice first and last
to see what it's trying to tell you.
Trust that it will guide you in the
right direction.
Learn to go by
your intuitive feelings
and don't be afraid
to express these feelings
if necessary.
The INNER YOU
is all you've got,
and
your 'little' voice is your guide.

Assertive

Being honest,
or being assertive,
means having the courage
to be yourself -
to show yourself
as you are
and not as you would
like people
to believe you are.

Song of Friendship

The person who has found a friend
has found a treasure.
A friend encourages and uplifts you
when you can only see the dark side
of everything you have ever done or
said.
They make you laugh
when you only want to moan and
groan
and take life seriously.
They supply insights of faith
when you feel you don't care
about anything.
And the best part of all is,
you can do the same for them
when they are going through
their rough patch.

Self-Possession

Self-possession comes about
after many efforts to
be in control
of every aspect of your life.
The experience of failure
helps you evaluate
what really matters:
the joyful doing of the work
rather than a successful outcome.
Although no one is going
to moan about being successful,
continuing to make efforts
when the
chips are down
turns
sand into gold.

Unique

You are a unique person.
The discovery of your own
uniqueness
is found when you begin
to love exactly who you are.
You are the only one of your kind.
An original.
The discovery of
your unique potential
is made through love.
So, love the things that make you
unique.
Your looks, your gifts and talents,
your thoughts and ideas - everything.
Discovering and respecting
your own uniqueness
causes you to thoroughly respect
the dignity and uniqueness
of others.

Fun

My sister overheard two little girls
asking her two year old son
his name.
"Joshua," he replied.
"What's the little boy's name?"
enquired their mother.
"Dracula," chorused the
two little girls.

Relaxing is Healthy

Taking time for yourself,
finding peace in your own company
is time well wasted.
By spending time alone,
recollected,
you can reach into the deepest part
of yourself.
It is from there that
health,
happiness and harmony
all spring.

Empathy

To have
an understanding heart
and an
ability to empathise
with other
human beings
is one of
life's
greatest
qualities.

Enjoyment

You can find enjoyment
in everything you do
by focusing your attention
on the exact thing
you are doing
in the present moment,
and getting the most out of it.
When you do what you enjoy
you put your energy to
the best use.
Nothing is wasted.
The art of finding something good
in the seemingly bad things that
happen or have to be dealt with
makes you realise that
every cloud
has a silver lining.

Wonder

What a fascination is a child's sense of
wonder.
To a child everything is new and amazing.
It's tireless energy to explore the unknown,
take risks,
attempt the impossible, and survive,
is nothing short of miraculous.
The attractiveness of such a spirit
is obvious,
but not always possible to practise,
especially when one is heavily involved
in the critical adult world.
What is possible is to develop
a 'chosen' adventurous spirit,
a spirit that, intelligently, leads us to follow
our dreams, to think originally and
creatively about the ordinary things in our
lives. We can figure out how to do things
differently, go to places we have never
been, take new routes in life.
We may not be a child, but we can use our
intelligence to show us a whole new aspect
of ourselves we didn't know existed -
The wonder of being grown up.

Noises

When you are about to fall asleep and
suddenly hear
an irritating noise,
e.g. a dog barking,
rain dripping,
a nose snoring,
tell yourself how beautiful
the sound is.
Continue to tell yourself
how beautiful it is.
Before you know it
you've fallen asleep.

Ideals

The person who wants
to make a difference,
who quietly wants
to change the way things are, merely
by
having his/her own
set of ideals
and
never losing sight of them,
is an Inspiration.

Saying 'No'

The hardest thing in the world,
at times, is to say 'no'
to another person,
especially someone you like.
To successfully say 'no' without
hurting another person is a special
art,
and there are times when it just has to
be done.
We cannot always
be available for
others.
There are times when our own needs
take priority.
But if we are well in tune with
our deepest spirit
we will know exactly
how to
soften the blow
so no one gets hurt.

Change the World

Probably the best place to start
is on ourselves.
An easy place to begin in one way
and, in another way,
it can be hard.
There will, no doubt, be failure.
The important thing
is not to stay down for too long.
Remember your ideal,
pick yourself up again
and continue the fight.
No one ever changed the world
in one day.

Parcels

Open your
parcels and letters
slowly and gently,
not tearing at them,
Tearing at parcels puts up
blood pressure
and aggravates you no end.
Open each parcel
as you would like somebody
to open one
that you had sent them.
Stay recollected.
You will enjoy
the surprise
all the more.

Your Dream

The luckiest person in the world is
the one who has a dream.
Dreams are what lift you up
out of the mundane to great heights.
Everything is possible to the person
who has the faith to believe
that their dream will come true.
Dreams are part of the
indomitable human spirit.
A dream raises your spirits,
gives you positive vision,
shows what you can achieve
if you apply yourself.
No matter how fantastic
it may seem to you,
your dream is your lifeblood,
the food and drink of your mind.
Never give up dreaming.

Love Change

One of the greatest things
you can do for yourself
is to love yourself.
Love everything about yourself.
If you can fully accept yourself,
without wanting
to change anything,
you are well on the road
to happiness and peace of mind,
and change will come
effortlessly.

At times

There are times when women
bring out the best in men,
and men bring out the best in
women. If we tapped a little more
into this reality
life could be wonderful.

Follow your Star

Every person is special
with a unique set of original hopes
and ideas.
So, have the courage
to follow your own individual star.
Don't be afraid
where it may lead you
since the satisfaction that comes
from having tried to make a
difference will far surpass any fear
of failure
you may ever have had.
There are few joys
to be compared with
reaching for your own star.

Prepare

Preparation goes
a long, long way
to making life more enjoyable.
Preparation
means getting ready
well in advance of the event.
Overseeing, checking, writing a list.
No detail is too small to make ready,
and the time to do it is now.
Preparation means
being ready for that surprise
opportunity you hope will
present itself.

Fear

If you can, attempt one thing you
find difficult
or are afraid of, every day.
In that way, you may break loose
from a cumbersome comfort zone
and make life
very interesting for yourself.

Don't Dry Up

Love will never dry up
unless you stop giving it.
The more you give away
the greater the store of love
you will have.
The only thing you may take with
you when you die
is the love you have given away.

Master

You are the master
of your own universe.
What you put into it
you will get out of it.
Put a lot of love in
and you will get
more than a lot of love out.

Country Joy

At least once a week
go to a beautiful place in the country.
Breathe in the pure air,
enjoy the freedom
and peace of natural surroundings,
inhale the fragrance of the
whole countryside.
I guarantee you will feel
rejuvenated,
healed
and made anew.

Tune In

Tune into
the innermost part of your being,
the real you.
Where?
Listen in silence to your inner voice.

Prayer

Prayer
is the
language
of love
between
you
and
God.

Be a Friend

The Bible says
'He who has found a friend has
found a treasure'.
A listening heart
hears with
compassion and sympathy
the troubles
and
daily ups and downs of others.
Cultivate this heart if you
want to have friends.

Change

There are so many things in the world
we would like to change,
so many areas
where love could make a difference.
Instead of, perhaps, griping about the
lack of love and care in the world, it's
good to realise
that you <u>can</u> make a difference.
By setting aside a little time,
maybe every day,
to actually put some love into the
world,
you are making a huge contribution to
positive change.
How?
Be really kind to a neighbour.
Do something special for an
elderly person.
Forgive a hurt.
Be patient with your child.
Love yourself.
Enjoy what you do.
Be where you are.

Graciousness

Be a gracious receiver.
When someone offers you a gift,
receive it graciously.
If you can't accept it,
refuse it graciously.
Never make the bearer of a gift
or invitation feel bad.
They have reached out to you.
Your first concern should be to make
them feel good
because they took a risk and
reached out to
a fellow human being.

Relax

It's great when we can enjoy
everything we do
and are tuned in to our creative selves
Then we can give and receive love.
If this is not priority in our lives
then maybe we have lost touch with our
real selves.
And sometimes we do lose touch with
this most important part of ourselves.
We are no longer happy, and we need
to relax.
Relaxation is one way to get back in
touch with yourself, the real you.
Sometimes we are under the illusion that
we won't get anything done if we are too
relaxed. In fact, the opposite is true.
When you are relaxed you astonish
yourself with how much you get done.
To be relaxed means to
perform at optimum level.
Instead of doing what causes stress,
trying too hard to do something or to get
somewhere, do the exact opposite.
Relax.

Courage

Have the courage
to follow your heart.
Take time
to make a little difference
in the life
of another person.

Respect

Respect yourself and you will have
respect for the other person in the
relationship.
You are unique individuals
with different needs and tastes.
The only way
you can agree or amicably disagree
is to
communicate.
The basis for this communication
is knowing the truth about yourself.
This knowledge and subsequent
communication helps you
understand and accept
the other person.
Know your strengths
and weaknesses.
Love to know them both.
Then you will be free.

Loosen Up

A great way to loosen up and see
things from a completely different
angle is to spend some time
with a child.
Play with a child and you will
discover things about yourself that
you hadn't realised were in you.
You will remember amazing things
about your own childhood.
It is such a precious time, not only
revealing
the natural wisdom
of children -
but you will loosen up and
grow in wisdom yourself.

For the Impatient

If patience is a problem for you, always make sure you have something to do that absorbs your mind. Otherwise your impatience may drive you crazy.

For example, if being stuck in traffic is a problem, remember to have your favourite CDs with you. Enjoy them while you sit looking out at cars. Anything at all that can distract you from an annoying situation is worth employing.

The Now

Learn to enjoy each moment to the
full. Give up longing for the future
and delving into the past.
The past is dead and gone and
there's not much you can do about it.
You can, of course, learn from it.
The future you can't predict.
So, the only time you have is now.
Observe the Now fully and enjoy
every second of it. Don't so much
wonder how it should be
as how it is.

Speed

There's a right way
and a wrong way to do everything.
Do it the right way first.
It's quicker.

Insecurity

When we are weak, we are insecure,
we lack confidence and our
self-esteem can be low.
Then, we are dangerous to be with.
If we can be upfront with our partner
about exactly what we are
experiencing,
we have a chance of avoiding
unhappy arguments.

Sooner rather than later.

Laughter

Laughter is a spontaneous outpouring of the
heart which has been excited by something
surprising.
Laughter cuts through seriousness and
completely reduces one to a child,
a playful child with no worries,
complaints or negative feelings.
For a moment, it frees you to make
new decisions and commitments.
And you can carry these out
without feeling burdened.
It opens the heart
so that the real you can emerge
and play.
The you that perhaps is not often seen.
Laughter lightens the load we
sometimes put on ourselves.
And discharges those negative
experiences
which make it impossible
to see the bright side of life.

Step 'Out of Line'

Stepping out of line can be a bit
scary
and, at the same time,
a very refreshing experience.
It takes courage to take on board
new challenges.
But, if you want to see things from a
completely new perspective,
if you want to experience 'new life',
stepping out of line is necessary.
What's ahead?
That's what's exciting
about the whole procedure...

Leaving the Past

Sometimes when we leave
our past behind
we begin to
uncover
the gold mine
under
the memories
and prejudices
we have
shovelled out.

A Better World

If you're anxious to make
the world a better place,
start with the easiest and closest area
- yourself.
Sit down and see
in what way
you can change
yourself.

Hidden Treasures

A new path
may open to you.
Pray about whether you should
take it,
for
hidden treasures
may lie there.
And God may want
a new you to be made,
a you that would never have been,
but for the fact
that you accepted
the invitation.

Success

The only way
you can really get on with
anyone successfully
is to love them.
No matter what other
methods you employ to achieve the
same end,
none will work as effectively
as loving the person
who irritates, annoys
or just generally gets on your nerves.
After all it's what we are asked to do
as Christians -
love our neighbour as ourself.

Water

Water takes the shape of
whatever vessel it is put into, no matter
how small, how big or how awkward.
It fills out every shape it finds.
If we want to be able for the various
challenges life throws at us, we need to
become like water. We need to have a
positive attitude
to everything:
see the good heart
beneath the hard exterior,
the advantage when we get a 'no',
the opportunity knocking
in undesirable places.
Seeing the upside of everything
causes us to move like liquid
through life.
And normally counterproductive
experiences wash over us,
changing us as we need to be changed
so we never become
'old' or stagnant.

Stressed Out

If you feel
you are stressed out
and there's no way out
except to go on working,
then do everything very slowly and
deliberately,
paying attention to small details.
Your situation may have come about
because you were not centred.
Try to get back on track
by giving yourself
more time
to do the smallest task.
You'll find your
stress levels
will become lower.

Love

Loving another person
expands the soul,
gets rid of boredom,
puts a thrill into your life
and
awakens your intelligence.
But, above all,
it fills your heart with
joy.

Growth

Change is nearly always
stressful,
especially when we don't want it.
But there are times
when it is essential to change
because growth cannot take place
without it.
If we can get ourselves
to relax into every aspect
of the change we are
being exposed to,
it makes it a lot more
palatable.

Under the Weather

If you are feeling a little under the
weather, discouraged perhaps,
no real purpose in life,
then you're probably suffering the
effects of some negative force.
What you need is a blast
of the positive.
Where is it going to come from?
Your friends?
Your husband/wife?
One place you can definitely get it
from is yourself.
Try highlighting all the best aspects
of your life, and specifically replace
negative thoughts
with positive ones.
You'll know it's working when life
becomes interesting again, friends
seem more attractive,
and your job is more purposeful
than before.
Keep at it.

Forgetful?

If you are inclined to be forgetful,
tell someone.
Ask that person to remind you of
what you want
to remember.
You'll find
in 90% of cases
you will remember,
yourself.

Create Beauty

Beauty and God
go hand in hand.
Create some beauty
in
everything you do.
When you eat, speak, walk, work,
incline towards
what is
beautiful.
Beauty and truth
go hand in hand.

Honesty

Being honest about how
and what you feel
provides mental health.
The quicker you can be honest,
the quicker your chance of happiness.
Honesty means
you have nothing to hide,
therefore
your mind is totally uncluttered
and you can get on with
the business of love,
that which life
is ultimately all about.

Forgiving Relationships

Relationships are built on
forgiveness,
empathy and respect.
No person is perfect
and there are times
when we have done things
that we
regretted afterwards
and have
found forgiveness
from the people we've hurt.
It's easy to make mistakes
and it is wonderful to be forgiven,
but it is also important
to develop an ability
to forgive ourselves.
With this in place,
it makes it a lot easier
to forgive others.

A Parable

A truck
at the entrance to a tunnel
was in a terrible predicament.
It was too high to drive through.
Experts racked their brains
to solve the problem,
when a young girl piped up
'Let the air out of the tyres!'
It worked like magic.

Risks

Where there is the greatest risk
of appearing a fool
both to ourselves and others,
a time when we are most vulnerable,
that could be the time
the greatest profit is to be made.
Even though our enterprise may fail,
it is certainly not a failure to have
taken a chance.
It is a refreshing and rejuvenating
experience that can be looked back
on with enjoyment.
If our risk-taking turns out to
be a success,
well and good.
If not, we can always, if we wish,
stand in the wings and wait for
the next opportunity
to 'go on stage'.

Encouragement

There are times
when we don't need sympathy
and we certainly
don't need advice,
What we would love
is a bit of downright
encouragement.
The encouragement to
have another go,
to hang in there when the going gets
tough,
to stay focussed
and not to let go of our dreams.
Someone to say our efforts haven't
been wasted
and, most of all,
we need plenty of encouragement
simply to enjoy what we do.

Somewhere

Somewhere above
human reason, logic,
intellect and memory
is a place
where all hearts meet.
To get to that place
we need to put aside our
human inclinations and attitudes,
not forever,
but for the time we want to be united
with another person,
persons or with God Himself.
It is a place God would like
to bring us to,
constantly.
A place where we
breathe pure air,
see with a clear eye
and
love with a generous heart.

Make it work

To make any relationship work
takes time.
Having fun together
is a big part of it.
It just doesn't happen, however.
You have to make it happen.
How your relationship
is at this very moment
equals the efforts
you have
put into it.

Read the Signs

We are born
dignified human beings
with a unique 'sign-system' within us
and, if we go by it and read the
signs,
we will develop an inner sense of
wisdom about ourselves
and the world around us.
This 'sign-system'
or inbuilt intuitiveness
is an extraordinary gift.
It is an immediate insight
into what is right and wrong
and can be used to great benefit
in decision making.
We can draw on this hidden wisdom
any time we want.
How many times have you thought
to do something, and didn't go with
it for some reason,
only to find out afterwards that it
would have paid off had you taken
heed of the 'signs'?

Communication

To be able
to communicate
with another person
you need to spend
some quiet time together
in an atmosphere
of freedom and love.
It's a bit difficult
to open up to another person
if one of you is always going on
about something or other.
Take time off to be quiet
with one another.
Silent time together
can be very special.

Eat Healthy

Eat something healthy
e.g. fruit, a salad,
steamed vegetables,
every day,
maybe even twice a day.
You will feel much better as a result.
Healthful eating
contributes a lot
to feeling good
about yourself.

Creative Relaxation

Creative relaxation
is a time for
waiting and listening.
A time for
new ideas and inspirations.
It allows a little fresh air into your
system,
which may be needed
from time to time.
To be in a position to experience
new insights
we need to be able
to give ourselves to
quietness and solitude.
It is in these quiet times
that we get a break from the noise
and pressures of life.
We are able to connect with our
deeper selves and emerge from our
quietness fully rejuvenated,
ready to have another go
at our creative dreams.

Kindness

Kindness never goes astray.
It is always rewarded,
especially when you make efforts to
be kind in situations of
extreme pressure.
For example, when you are
extremely irritated
or angry with somebody,
kindness under this pressure
adds lustre and dignity to your soul.
Whatever about changing the other
person, you, yourself, are
being changed for the better.
And that is a wonderful reward.

Harmony

The ability
to harmonise
with others
comes from being
happy with ourselves,
playing our own tune.
Everyone has something
they don't like about themselves,
but the person who accepts and
puts their flaws in the background
and chooses rather to perform
what they simply are,
their transparent, honest self,
easily harmonises with others.
If you love
who and what you are,
harmony
will definitely
come
your way.

The 'Mark' System

The 'mark' system
for disciplining children goes
something like this:
a good mark for the good things
they do,
a bad mark for the naughty things.
So many bad marks equal a suitable
discipline, e.g. no TV for a day, a
week, or no special treat after dinner.
So many good marks equal a movie,
perhaps, or a really nice treat.
This special system helps you
to objectively discipline your
children with love
without having to go into a frenzy
whenever
they do something wrong.
It also involves them in being
responsible for their own choices.

Friendship

Friendship
is about
sharing a moment together,
a unique moment
with
another person.
That two people
of completely different minds
can come together
and agree on anything
is actually
a phenomenon.
To be able to sustain
that for any length of time
is nothing short
of a
miracle.

One Thing

Don't try to do two things
at the same time.
You probably won't be able
to do justice
to either of them.
Just one thing at a time.

Don't Share

When you are about to make
a commitment of some kind,
don't make the mistake
of sharing it.
Sometimes,
when you share it, you get
so much negative input
that it causes you
to waver and wonder if you should
go ahead.
At this important time,
listen to your inner self,
your inner voice,
that Presence inside which knows
what you should and shouldn't do.
It doesn't mean you
won't take advice from others.
Just don't tell them the whole story
until you have finally decided
on what you want to do.

Alone Time

Give those you love
time to be alone.
Everyone needs
their own
space.
You love others
by being happy for them
when they leave,
and happy when they return.

A Healthy Ear

Your health
depends
to a large extent
on having
healthy relationships
with the people
you are surrounded by
everyday.
Every one of those relationships
is different,
every person needing
to be loved
in a different way.
How you get on depends on how
and what you listen to
coming from the mouth of each one.

A Challenge

Is there something
that always excited your interest,
that you always wanted to learn?
Challenge yourself
to
learn it.

Innate Goodness

Believe in yourself.
Believe in your innate goodness
and you'll find you will be filled
with faith, hope and love
for all the things you want to achieve.

Within Us

Within each one of us there is a
'church'
where we can go for comfort,
rest and reflection.
It is, at times, vital for us
to discover this place in ourselves.
It's the place God has made
for us to retreat to
when things are not going
so well in the physical world.
We are rejuvenated here,
strengthened
and given back our
sense of equilibrium
to venture out into the world
once more
full of new love and
expectation.

Citizens of Heaven

Perhaps a friend needs help.
Is there someone to forgive?
A friendship to be renewed?
A broken promise to be mended?
A daughter or son to be
reconciled with?
An uncle or aunt to love?
There may be dark areas in our lives
where we can open up and and let the
light of human and divine love
shine in,
thereby transforming us into suitable
citizens for
our heavenly paradise.

Being on Time

One of the kindest things
we can do for our neighbour
is to be on time.
Punctuality
inspires an enormous amount
of good will.
It tells a lot about the character
of the person who is punctual.
It's not the easiest thing,
being on time,
since so many things
need looking after
just as we are about
to leave for an appointment.
But so much trust
depends on it
nowadays,
who can afford to be late?

Loving Friends

Spend together-time
with the one you love, very often.
Spend time in each others arms,
simply enjoying
the warmth of the other person.
Doing nothing,
going nowhere,
no deadlines,
no hidden agenda.
Just peace.

Comfort Zone!

We all need a comfort zone.
It makes us feel secure
and safe.
The only problem is
sometimes our comfort zone
makes other people
feel uncomfortable,
even hurt.
So, comfort zones have to be
carefully examined
and maybe adjusted
so that
we find our safety
in the widest embrace.

Caught Up

Sometimes we get caught up
with things that don't matter
and leave the
really important things
to fall by the wayside.
For example, when we get
really interested in something,
or somebody, and something goes
wrong, we get hurt
and immediately might
take ourselves very seriously.
We withdraw from life
and make it difficult for people
to communicate with us.
This may be a growth process
whereby we learn that nothing
is worth taking
<u>that</u> seriously.
Our prime concern must be love,
people, God.
What else is there?

Help!!

Some people would rather drown
than shout for help.
Asking for help is a sign that we
are weak and not totally sufficient
in ourself.
Who is?
Better to humble oneself
and be free from a burden
than to carry it around
along with the false illusion
that it isn't heavy.

Good Ideas

Instead of putting
all the good ideas
you get on the long finger,
experiment with one or two.
Try them out.
Perhaps, in no time,
you'll discover
a hidden talent.
Imagine going through life
with a set of marvellous talents
you didn't even know you had!
How do you uncover what's there?
Those good ideas that cross your
mind
may be the key.
Start small,
explore an idea you think is really
worthwhile.
You may just have the goods
to make it come true.

Does God Care?

God cares about everything,
'the little no less than the great'.
He cares about healing people,
about lifting a donkey
out of a ditch on Sunday.
He knows every hair on your head,
every breath you take,
every beat of your heart.
He notices
and strongly supports
every time you reach out to another.
Every time you care.

Easy Prayer

For the person
who finds prayer
a difficulty,
try simply
to sit in silence
and 'look'
at God.
Contemplative prayer
is mostly
opening our hearts
to Him,
without thinking
or
speaking.

Take Time Off

Our negative thoughts
and emotions are bound to wear us
down.
And if not us, our nearest neighbours.
An interesting practice is to have
a Positive Day,
a day when you do not allow yourself
breathe one negative word,
think one negative thought,
cultivate one negative emotion.
God is good. He truly wants us to be
happy. All the time.
It is we who have invented the
Theology of Gloom.
Spend one day only seeing the
Goodness of God
in all things.
You'll be surprised.

Creative Time

We need to give
our creative nature
an outlet.
We definitely should have a
Creative Time
every day, or at least once a week
where we can
simply be creative.
Play on an instrument,
paint,
sing,
dance,
draw.
No barriers, rules, thoughts, fears.
Free exploration.
Trust your feelings and instincts,
don't look for approval
from anyone.
Let the artist in you
loose.

Fear of Mistakes

Cultivate the attitude of
being in charge of every aspect
of your life.
Make decisions.
Set things in motion.
People who are afraid to make
mistakes have already made the
biggest one possible.
They sentence themselves to a
term of boredom.
Our capacity is much bigger than we
think and few of us even begin to tap
into the vastness of it.
It's interesting that many of the
greatest minds in the planet's history
were regarded in their time as
a bit 'off the beam'.
Now, we call them geniuses.
Thank God they weren't put off
by the wagging tongues
and fashionable opinions
of those who knew better.

'Fess Up'

It's a sort of emotional relief
to be able to be honest about your
past.
It can also be interesting, the course
a person takes to be free
- admitting past wrong-doings.
It makes one wonder about the
benefits of 'confession',
how facing one's skeletons
and relating them to a confessor frees
one from all guilty feelings,
making it possible to start afresh.
Nowadays, we have the option to
pay the psychiatrist
or
visit a confessor.

A Healing Heart

A healing heart is
gentle,
understanding,
non-judgemental,
open,
honest
and
free.
It listens.
Says little.
Loves much.

Send Love

It's hard to extend
the hand
of forgiveness
to your oppressor,
to absorb a hurt
and let
bygones be bygones.
Pause a moment
and
reflect.
God is the Healer.
Through you He can send
Divine Love
into the heart of
your oppressor.

Thank You

Think about all the people
that have helped you to love.
Think about all the people
you have loved in the past.
Say a silent prayer of thanks
to them
for allowing you
to love them,
for all
the happiness they've brought
into your life.

Deep Faith

Can you see the insecure child behind
the macho tough guy?
The wounded heart within
the angry housewife?
The confusion, frantic grasping
of the know-all?
God can.
The world of faith is a world
of pity.
God loves us because we are
so helpless.
It is indeed a deep faith that is able to
see what God and our deep heart
understands.

To Love or Be Loved?

Which is better - to love or be loved?
By nature we crave to be loved
and, if we do not receive love,
we become damaged in some way.
But, what if you feel
no one loves you?
The Gospel answers this problem
by exhorting each of us to love.
'Love one another
as I have loved you'.
'Love your neighbour as yourself'.
Perhaps our loneliness is cured by
going out and relieving the loneliness
of others.
Perhaps when we love others as
much
as they need,
we in turn will be loved
as much as we need.

Release the Hurt

Hurts can manifest themselves
in different parts of the body.
When somebody hurts you
it can literally 'get your back up',
so you find that you may have pains in
the upper part of your shoulders
and neck.
When the hurt is resolved
you'll find that you are more able to relax
that part of your body.
Maybe even be pain free.
The secret is relax, forgive
and release the hurt.
Talk yourself through it.
'I release the pain in my...(mention it)'.
Imagine it leaving your body.
Let it go. It's false protection to keep it.
Rather, decide to face the cause of it and
cure it at the source.
Forgive the cause so that
your encounter with it will be loving
and not revengeful.

Jobs

Want to feel good about
yourself?
Do the jobs
you hate to do, first.
Get them out of the way.
Then you'll be free
to enjoy
everything else you do
for the rest
of the
day.

Sleep

Sleep is a great healer.
Give yourself
the luxury of a few
early nights every week.
It can make a noticeable difference
to your energy levels.
Both
spiritually
and
physically
you'll feel much better.

Make a List

Making a list is one of
the best ways to get things done.
Have a notebook and pen always at
hand to write down inspirations,
ideas, jobs to be carried out, etc.
It doesn't matter how long the list
gets.
Tackle each job on the list,
one at a time.
Review your list at a set time.
You can be sure that,
once you adhere to the list method,
each item will definitely be seen to.

The Present Moment

To live in
the present moment
is to be a fully alive human being.
To be aware of
exactly where you are and
what you're doing
takes time and practice.
Sometimes
we are present only in body;
our mind is totally
somewhere else.
To enjoy the fullness
of the present moment
and receive all the riches
it has to give us
requires that we are fully present
to it,
body, mind and spirit.

Environment

Every little thing we do
has an effect on the environment.
If we throw our papers on the street,
we are rid of them,
but the environment suffers.
Carelessness leads to
plastic bags in trees and bushes,
clogged drains and
polluted rivers.
Do what you can
to make up for any
environmental transgression
you may have committed.

Plant a tree.

Reflect

Reflection
can be a great way
of
assessing a situation.
Once you have reflected, you can
then decide on
your
plan of action.

Embarrassing Moments

Our tendency, when we have
an embarrassing moment,
is to hide it and try to forget it
as quickly as possible.
Understandable.
Yet, embarrassing moments revealed
can set us free from
the fear of what 'everyone thinks'.
It's certainly good to relate it
to a friend afterwards.
It can be a great source of fun
and we are released from
the burden of its memory.

Neighbours

No matter how hard we try, we just
can't get away from our neighbour.
Our neighbour needs our heart,
our appreciation, our love.
It's where happiness lies,
this doing and being something
for our neighbour.
We may have a problem
with certain neighbours and decide
to move somewhere else,
but there will be another neighbour there who may drive us just as
demented.
The problem lies within ourselves.
A popular song puts it this way,
"If you want to make the world a
better place take a look at yourself
and change'.
We may just keep meeting those
annoying types until we make some
alteration in ourselves.
Then they seem to be nicer people.

Learning Relaxation

Choose a beautifully remote place,
pretty and quiet.
Inhale the aroma of your surroundings.
Listen to the ambient sounds.
Breathe deeply.
Allow all the delicate perfumes
to fill your spirit.
Breathe.
Breathe in relaxation.
Breathe out tension.
Let go of all worries
and non-essentials.
Relax every part of your body.
Slowly become aware of the parts where
you experience tension.
Gently move and relax those parts.
Breathe in the whole experience of nature
that makes you feel at home and at ease.
When your time is up,
come slowly and quietly back into the
'active' world, bringing
peace and restfulness with you.

A Cat Nap

Take a nap
when you really need it.
A short period of sleep
for 10 to 15 minutes
can make a huge difference
to your
mental alertness.
You wake up
refreshed and ready
to tackle
the workload
again.

Don't go it alone

You may have a really great idea or
concept, but be stuck at a particular
point.
Although you feel you want to
develop
the idea alone, this may just not be
possible. Perhaps you're lacking in
finances or a particular ability,
and the project stops there.
Look around for someone
trustworthy who is sufficiently
equipped
to help you make it all happen.
This may add a whole new
dimension
of fresh encouragement and 'go'.
The inspiration may be a 'symphony'
in its own way.
Do what you do best
and call in the other players.

Swear Words

The easiest habit in the world
to pick up is
cursing,
usually when something
unpleasant
happens to us.

Not to swear
is another choice.

Counting Blessings

The best time
to count your blessings
is when you feel
you have nothing
to be grateful for.
When you feel you're in a slump.
Start with all the things
you take for granted:
'Thanks for having a dinner today.
Thanks for having a pair of shoes.
Thanks for water coming out of
the tap.
Thanks for... '
It's easy to see how much there is
to be grateful for.
There is so much to appreciate
we normally wouldn't even
think about.
And it's just a choice to do so.

Spreading Peace

Wars begin and end in the heart of
one person.
You'll more than likely find one
name
prominently attached
to every major upheaval
since the beginning of time.
Also, every great peace movement
was probably initiated by one person.
When you feel annoyance
in your heart towards someone,
there's a potential war brewing.
Choose peace.
Choose to spread peace.
One act of peace
contributes enormously
to the peace of the world.

Recycle It!

Recycle
what you can.
But don't kill yourself
trying to recycle absolutely
everything.
It might just become
an obsession
and you'll be an annoying bore
to yourself and others.
It's like the person who wants to
wash the dishes
before he has eaten the meal.
Preserve, first,
the joy
in
what you do.

Heart Intention

The value of a thing
very much equals
the integrity of the intention.
God looks at the heart
of a person,
not so much at their actions
or the outcome of their actions.
Look into your heart.
What's there?
That's who you are.
Once the heart is right
everything
is right.
And everything
falls into place
as it should.

Drive

Go for
a long drive
at least once a month
with a loved one,
and allow the
conversation
to flow.
A great aid
to
communication
and
togetherness.

Tease

Never
tease another person
in a bad way,
especially
the person you love.
But you can
tease a person in a good way
and
have a
lot of fun.
Be careful, though.

See the Good

Always
try to see
the good.
Put a good motive
on what others do.
It will pay off in the long run.
Never accuse another person
of having
a bad
motive.

Skills

Relaxation
plays a big part
in the
acquiring of many skills.
The more relaxed
we are the better
we're able to take in
the knowledge we need.
When we are relaxed
our thinking powers are clearer
and more alert,
yet not in any stressful way.
Science has proved
that non-intrusive nature sounds
or gentle classical music,
together with
deep relaxation,
allow you
take in more information, faster,
and retain it longer,
than conventional methods
of learning.

Bad News

Bad news is depressing
so why listen to it?
For one day a week
cut out listening to the news
and reading newspapers
and see does it make a difference
in your life.
You could be really daring and
try a whole week.
It's easier to listen
to the gentle voice of your own heart
when sensational, outside distractions
are kept at a minimum.

Your Mission

You have an original contribution to
make to the world
and the sooner you get started
the better.
Making this unique contribution
will bring you and the Earth
an enormous amount of peace and
fulfilment.
Find out exactly what God
wants you to do.
Pray about your mission in life,
why you yourself are here.
But let your prayer be
without pressure.
The world responds
more favourably
to the embrace of love
and the world is waiting
for your contribution.

What Do You Love?

If you
love what you do
you'll be good at it.
You may not
be brilliant
straight off,
but that will come
with time
and
perseverance.
It is extremely
healthy
to love what you do.
Placing your focus
in your area
of strength
creates a feeling
of well-being
and a
pressureless atmosphere.

The Call Within

The world becomes a better place
when any woman or man
takes up the challenge
to try and create
what they feel inside themselves.
When they
respond to the call within
for higher and better things,
when they try to put a form on the
vision they see inside.
Don't ever short-change yourself
with excuses like 'I'm too young
or I'm too old
to do that'.
If you have a heart
you're the right age.

No Free Lunches

Although it might appear to be
a very simplistic way of looking
at life,
it is true to say that the secret of life
is
'There are no free lunches'.
No matter what we want to do
there is a price to pay.
So, we can pay up happily
or grumble and complain.
It doesn't take away from the fact
that
nothing is handed to us
on a silver platter.
Shakespeare has a very positive take
on it:
'Joy's soul lies in the doing.'

Goal Management

'It's a goal!!!'
How often have we heard that
on TV, radio or in the live setting.
We are goal-oriented creatures,
loving to pit our wits
against a challenge,
overcome and win.
All ego aside, this goal scoring
keeps us alive and kicking
and is an undoubted
source of enjoyment to be nurtured.
Provided we can manage it
and it doesn't take over our lives.
The first important step is to
write down all your goals:
Your life goal,
personal goals,
business goals.
Start thinking about how to
score each of them.
Methodically.
Enjoy the game!

The New

The new always disturbs
because change has to take place
to make way for it.
When a 'new baby' arrives,
everything is pushed aside
for this new life.
A new life needs special attention
so that it can survive
in the early months of its existence.
Your life,
your surroundings
will never be the same again
because of it.
Everything is different.
You have begun a new
and adventurous life-journey
because you made way for
this 'new birth'.

Going to Bed

The state of your mind when you
go to bed
will be the state of your mind
when you arise the next morning.
If you want to wake up feeling
refreshed and ready
for the new day,
try to 'wind down' before going to bed.
Read gentle poetry,
drift to sleep listening to
relaxing music,
or,
as you did when you were a child,
say your prayers.

They <u>do</u> love me

Don't believe it when you think
or feel that a friend doesn't love you
any more.
Believe the opposite
and it will come true.
Believing others love you
swells your heart,
making you want to love them.
They, in turn, will pick up
your good vibes
and will respond to you.
Lovingly.

Facing Yourself

Facing yourself
exactly as you are
with weaknesses, faults, etc.
and trying to do
something positive about them
takes a lot of courage.
It can help to consider using your energy
wisely.
This means understanding how
being bad tempered,
self-confused,
downright stubborn, over shy,
over pressured,
etc, etc,
is simply wasting your energy
and making your world miserable.
Losing your temper for even a short time
can use up all your emotional energy
for one day.
Then you have no reserves left to
appreciate the numerous unexpected
things
that are designated to come your way.

Food

Whatever you want to do in life,
you must think about what you can
eat that will support your activity.
Nutrition and nutrition in relation
to health (as opposed to tablets,
drugs and injections)
is a big, and often
controversial subject.
Some would say, you live or die,
depending on what you eat.
Food, and even health, cannot be
an end in itself, however.
The purpose for which you eat and
want to be healthy is what counts.
Bear in mind the type and degree
of activity
you wish to undertake
and for how long,
and eat whatever will
best keep you performing
optimally.

Check It

If possible, never do
anything important
on the spur of the moment.
Check things thoroughly,
or, better still,
if you're not sure,
have somebody else check them for
you as well.
Mistakes can easily go undetected
especially when you are
in too much of a hurry
to get something done.
What difference will
another hour, day or even week
make,
in terms of time,
when the final outcome
may have to last forever?

Indicators

The experience of pain in your body
is a fair indication
that something is wrong.
Perhaps physically,
perhaps even psychologically.
Emotional hurt is a good indicator
that something needs fixing,
maybe at the self-worth level.
Indicators are usually quick
to kick in,
so it isn't normally difficult
to ascertain the cause of an upset.
Some indicators, though, take
a long time to make their presence felt,
if you're not so sensitive to them.
You know, if you want something
too much,
the little inkling that it may be
dangerous, for example,
is not as loud as the desire
to race ahead of the traffic
and be in time.
You learn by experience.

Neat

Although neatness
can appear to be boring at times,
it does make you feel good,
overall.
And it really pays off
when you are in a hurry
to find something.

Another Way

What doesn't come with
a certain ease,
especially if you are
relaxed and enthusiastic,
forget about.
Try something else
or
try another way.

Send Flowers

Always go with those inspirations
to write a letter,
make a phone call
or send flowers.
This is how you show someone
they are special.
And not only do you brighten up
their life,
you brighten up your own, as well.

21 Days

Our choices make us what we are.
We are the way we are now
because we have
chosen the circumstances
that have put us in this position.
If we want things to be different
we have to make
different choices.
Nothing happens
unless we want it to happen.
We must start the ball rolling.
It is said that it takes
21 days to establish a new habit.
If you begin now
to change or acquire a new skill,
it will take about 21 days
to set it
firmly in place.
Not a long time.

Antidote for Jealousy

Mature love is very hard to come by,
but it is something worth aiming for.
We have a natural inclination to love;
we also have a natural inclination
to be jealous.
Sometimes the reason we are jealous
of another person is because we would
like to have what they have
or be what they are.
Loving to be yourself,
to be what you are,
very often helps
re-balance your sense of security.
If you've flaws, try to readily admit
them and honestly admire
the opposite qualities in the
person you are jealous of.
Be friendly with this person.
You're really doing well when you've
both become so friendly that they're
giving you tips on
how to improve in the area you're
lacking.
Full marks for that!

Inspiration-Catching

Inspirations cannot be ordered,
but you can condition yourself to
receive them by creating a
receptive atmosphere around
yourself.
How many times have you had
an inspiration,
but didn't have pen and paper ready
to write it down?
Inspirations captured create
a capacity for more.
They are hard to catch and hold
because they're like tiny whispers,
barely 'audible'
and totally pressureless.
Always be ready with pen and paper,
or your phone.

Inspirations,
they don't hang around.

Bumpy Ride

Life is a bumpy ride,
but if you
hold on tight
to Humility,
keep your head down
and have a
Sense of Humour,
you will
always
come out
on
top.

Healing Hands

Lay your hands on the part of your
body that is sick.
Love the sick part of your body.
Treat it kindly and gently.
God has given you
this little cross
to lead you
closer
to
Light, Love and Truth.

Selective TV

Be selective about what you
watch on TV.
Everything you watch has an
effect on you.
Violent programmes might make you
irritable during the day.
Negative programmes may leave you
grumbling about this and that.
Having watched the screen,
monitor yourself to see how you are
as a result of your choices.
The first few minutes of any show
generally give you the tone
of the rest of it.
Be in charge.

Viruses

There are times when you feel
you are going crazy.
You may feel weak, out of sorts
and extremely irritated with
everything
and
everybody,
especially those you love.
All that may be wrong is you've
picked up a little virus.
If so, there's nothing more
to worry about
except to take time off
and look after yourself
with lots of love,
care and plenty of rest.
Those little creatures
were made to help us
restructure our life-priorities,
or just give us time
to read a good book.

More about Failures

If you don't have any failures
to your credit
you haven't really been trying
hard enough.
The road to success is paved with
failures;
the more failures,
the more you have been trying.
If you want to be a success,
get out there
and clock up a few failures.

The Window Box

If you can't have a garden,
why not have a window box?
Or a hanging basket?
God created flowers
to cheer up
a colourless heart.

Soul Mate

We are hardly ever complete
on our own.
Whether we like it or not,
we need others.
We need at least one good friend
to be complete.
Being with your soul mate is one
of the greatest joys in life.
Never stop looking.
Never settle for second best.

Impossible?

Doesn't matter who tells you
'it's impossible',
for the person who believes
everything and anything
is possible.
If you can think it up
it can be done.

The Presence of God

Retire to a quiet place where you
can be alone.
Place yourself in the Presence
of God.
He is within and without you.
Healing you.
We are all in great need of healing.
Your silence in the Presence of God
can bring this about effortlessly.
By handing yourself over to God,
the Healer,
you open yourself to be filled with
His love.
When you leave your quiet place,
it will be as a person
full of peace.

LIFE

You are in charge of your life.
You make it or break it.
What you don't have control over
are outside circumstances,
but what you can control
is your attitude to everything
that happens.

About the Author

Gabrielle Kirby, Artist and Author, is best known for her popular range of Relaxation CDs and Videos.
Her Art Photography greeting cards are much sought after for that special someone.
Originally from Dublin, she now lives in Wicklow, Ireland.

Email: gabriellekirby@gmail.com

www.gabriellekirby.com

Books by Gabrielle Kirby

You Can Heal Your Self - I Did!
New Reflections

GREETING CARDS

Inspirational
Nature
Celtic
Birthday
Sympathy

By Gabrielle Kirby

CDs
Let's Relax
Super Relaxation
Meditation
Heal Your Self
The Power of the Present Moment
Thoughts to Power your Day
Thoughts to Power your Life
Glendalough - a Celtic Journey
Bereavement
Ecstasy of the Moment
Respond to your Heart
Solving All Problems
Let's Be Assertive
Let Go of Jealousy
Encourage Yourself

CHILDREN
Nóilín and the Leprechaun

DVDs
Let's Relax
Peaceful Meditation
Glendalough - a Mystical Journey